Baby

E N G L I S H

A dictionary for interpreting the secret language of infants

by Bill Adler, Jr.,
and Karen Adler

Illustrated by Bonnie Timmons

POCKET BOOKS

New York   London   Toronto   Sydney   Tokyo   Singapore

An *Original* Publication of POCKET BOOKS

 POCKET BOOKS, a division of Simon & Schuster Inc.
1230 Avenue of the Americas, New York, NY 10020

Copyright © 1993 by Adler & Robin Books, Inc.
Illustrations copyright © 1993 by Bonnie Timmons

ISBN: 0-671-79503-1

First Pocket Books trade paperback printing November 1993

10 9 8 7 6 5 4 3 2 1

POCKET and colophon are registered trademarks of
Simon & Schuster Inc.

Printed in the U.S.A.

To Matti (Madeleine)
and
Nessa (Vanessa), Karen's cousins

Acknowledgments

On the adult side, Peggy Robin and Liz Prungel gave much thought to the words that babies understand—and don't. Most of the credit for this book, however, goes to the under twenty-four-month-old crowd: Madeleine Adler Harrington, Vanessa Robin, Cara Vogel Appelstein, Rose Zion Malloy, Elizabeth Weiss, Rose Douglas, and Karen's playmates at the NCRC, Macomb Street, and Woodley playgrounds. Of course, a few grown-ups at Pocket Books helped, too, including Claire Zion, Tammy Fergus, and Angela Kyle. As did Joanna Robin, Richard Robin, and Karen's grandparents, Bill, Gloria, Florence, and David.

Introduction

"Kakool."

Ever wonder what that means? Or "s . . . s . . . s"? Or "muk"? These are baby-words. They are part of Baby-English, a language understood clearly by children under the age of two, and understood almost not-at-all by adults and older children.

To further communication between babies and parents, we developed this foreign-language dictionary to translate between Baby-English and adult English. It's simple to use: Just look up the word that sounds like what your baby has uttered, and you'll find a list of definitions, including some of the more obscure meanings that the word may have. Because the same word may be pronounced differently by different babies, look up the most likely sounding word and see if that matches what your son or daughter has said. We have provided alternative pronunciations where we have uncovered them.

Baby-English is also an invaluable lexicon for grandparents and frequent visitors of parents with small children. Ever gone to somebody's house and been stumped how the parents can understand the seemingly nonsensical sounds that the young ones speak? The parents have had plenty of practice translating Baby-English; with this dictionary now you can understand what your friends' children are saying.

As children acquire vocabulary, they try out all sorts of sounds and combinations of sounds, just to see what effect these proto-words have on you. If *caeeoo* results in your picking him up, then *caeeoo* now means "pick me up." It's a brand-new word for you and your baby.

The second part of the book is a lexicon of English to Baby-English. Why include this dictionary? Well, if you've ever questioned why your baby doesn't seem to respond to a particular word, just look up that English word to see what it really means to your baby.

There's one other thing that we want to say about this book: Have fun reading it. We had fun compiling it.

PART 1

A Baby-English Dictionary

There are two important differences between Baby-English and adult English. The first is the vocabulary. The second is the grammar.

Diphthongs, contractions, and other phonetic aberrations are practically impossible for many babies. But that doesn't stop them from trying. What comes out of their mouths may not resemble any sounds you are accustomed to, but with a little effort and imagination, it's possible to translate these utterances into adult language. A single word in Baby-English may translate into an entire complex sentence in adult English. After all, if a baby can't manage to string more than a few syllables together, then that baby is going to make the most efficient use of those syllables.

Parts of speech in Baby-English also differ from adult English. For example, Baby-English has what we call "transient verbs," which are used until a child is about three years old. Transient verbs express time components in durations under five minutes. Some transient verbs express time in less than thirty seconds.

Examples of transient verbs include *boon* (let the balloon fly away, then get it back) and *caeeoo* (carry me for an indefinite but short period of time).

A slight majority of nouns in Baby-English are comprehensive nouns; in other words, when a baby specifies "book," she wants *all* the books. On the other hand, she may want a particular book, such as *Goodnight Moon* and may keep saying "no" as you produce various books until you give her the right one. Unfortunately there's no part of Baby-English that is used to distinguish between the two.

There's a conundrum about Baby-English. Often it's difficult to distinguish between when a toddler says something because she wants it, and when she says something because she likes the way it sounds. This problem has led many a parent to prepare an entire meal, only to discover that Junior just enjoys the sound "meeet."

How, then, do you tell the difference between something wanted and something merely uttered? Even the fact that a baby repeats a particular word over and over again doesn't guarantee that she wants that thing. One way is to listen to the rhythm of your child's speech. While being repeated, if the word in question becomes higher in pitch or is shortened, that's an indication that the word is being said for a purpose, not for entertainment. For example, "Meeet, meeet, meeet, meeet" could mean "I like to say *meat*" or it could mean "I want meat." (If it's the latter, you'll know soon.) But "meet, meet, mít" means "I've got to have that meat now!"

But this is not a grammar book. (Phew.) At this juncture we just wanted to introduce you to the concept of transient verbs, comprehensive nouns, and other parts of baby-speech. It's useful to keep in mind that Baby-English doesn't always work the same way that adult English does.

Every toddler is different. Pay close attention to intonation in your baby's speech. Often that provides a large clue to the meaning of a particular word.

â Verb: 1. *please pick this up for me* 2. *I will pick this up.* Adjective: *nice.*

ahm Also pronounced **ahma, ama, hamme.** Noun: 1. *home* 2. *mom or dad's office* 3. *grandparents' house* 4. *wherever the car stops.*

appull Also pronounced **appool, ap.** Noun: *apple.* Also means: 1. *peach* 2. *pear* 3. *food of any kind* 4. *colored tennis ball.*

arf   arf   arf

arf Noun: 1. *dog* 2. *bear* 3. *seal.* (See WOOF)

ât Also pronounced **æht, hut,** or **hat.** Noun: 1. *there is a hat* 2. *any object placed on top of a head, including a stuffed animal or diaper* 3. *the uppermost* *object in a given pile* 4. *lampshade.* Verb: 1. *put my hat on* 2. *take my hat off* 3. *I want your hat.*

awá-u Verb: *go away.*

awl-dun Adjective: 1. *I'm tired of playing with this toy* 2. *I'm tired of holding this bottle* 3. *I don't want to look at the food on my tray anymore.* Verb: *you are done eating and will now play with me.*
(See DURTEE)

awl-gone Also pronounced **allll-gun, hall-gon, owl-gun.** Noun: 1. *I'm done drinking or eating* 2. *I want something else to eat or drink* 3. *I know what this stuff is in the bottle; it's called "all gone"* 4. *(seldom) all gone.*

ba Also pronounced **beeeee, b, buh, banke, bakke, bankie, oh-bee**. Noun: only known meaning, *blanket*.

baal Noun: 1. *ball* 2. *orange* 3. *grape*.

ba – ba   ba – ba   ba – ba

ba-ba Noun: 1. *sheep* 2. *large, furry dog* 3. *Barbara*.

baby Also pronounced **baabeee**. Noun: most common meaning, *any person under four feet tall*. Also means *me*. Frequently used to describe children up to the age of four, much to their dismay.

baggie Noun: 1. *diaper bag (place where there are some toys, some Cheerios, and possibly some milk available)* 2. *a plastic Baggie that contains Cheerios*.

bak Verb: *make this the way it was (as in "put the baby kangaroo back in its pouch," "put the page I ripped out back in the book").*

bakkey Verb: *put me in the laundry basket and push me around the room.*

bal Noun: *bottle.* Verb: *I want milk.* (See MUK)

bat Verb: *1. I want a bath 2. I want to see you get wet again.*

bayoo Noun: *berry.*

bear Noun: *1. bear 2. my favorite stuffed animal 3. dog or any large, furry animal 4. daddy.*

Bi-ba Also pronounced **Bi-Bir**. Noun: *Big Bird (from "Sesame Street").*

bie-bie Noun: *good-bye.*

bie-bie-u Verb: *go away!*

b e a r

bo Noun: *a bow.* Verb: *please put my hat on.*

boo Adjective: 1. *blue* 2. *any color.*

bood Also pronounced **bud, tweet**. Noun: 1. *bird* 2. *any animal that whistles.*

1.

2.

boom-boom Adverb: *I fell, but it wasn't serious.*
(See BOOM-BOOM in English-Baby section)

boon Noun: *balloon*. Verb: *make this balloon fly away, then I want it back.*

bow-wow Noun: meanings include: 1. *bear* 2. *my favorite stuffed animal.*

brak-brak

brak-brak

brak-brak Also pronounced **peep-peep**. Noun: *chicken.*

bud Also pronounced **but, bat**. Verb: 1. *I want to get into the bed with you* 2. *I'm extraordinarily tired and want to nap.*

buddy Also pronounced **numma** and (seldom) **bûnnie**. Noun: *rabbit*. (See RABBI)

buk Noun: 1. *book* 2. *greeting card* 3. *catalog*. Verb: *turn the pages*. Not to be confused with **muk**, which can sound the same when uttered by a baby in distress.

buk-buk Verb: *read to me*. (See REEDA)

But Noun: *Bert* (as in Bert from "Sesame Street").

bye-bye Also pronounced **byyy**, **bie-ba**. Imperative verb: *You! Wave hands.*

b y e b y e

caeoo

caeoo Verb: *carry me.*

Cat↑

cat Also pronounced **garow**. Noun: most common meaning, *cat*. In babies under one year, may also mean: 1. *dog* 2. *horse* 3. *large bird* 4. *squirrel* 5. *other mammals* (See MEOW)

ches Noun: *cheese*.

cumptr Noun: *piano*.

da-da Noun: 1. *the male parent* 2. *for babies under one year, any male who appears, including the plumber, postman, and taxi driver.*

da-da, da-da Verb: *Daddy, play with me.*

14

da-da, da-da, da-da Verb: *Daddy, I need you to get me my toy.*

da-dee Also pronounced **di-da**. Noun: *male parent only.*

da-dit Noun: 1. *daddy* 2. *somebody who resembles daddy.*

da-ma Noun: most common meaning 1. *any parent—quick!* Also means, 2. *mommy* 3. *daddy.*

dansse Verb: 1. *let's boogie* 2. *hold my hands and swing me around* 3. *let's play ring-around-the-rosy.*

dare Noun: 1. *bear* 2. *chair* 3. *stairs.*

dat Noun: 1. *I want that thing* 2. *I have something important to say and why can't you understand what "dat" means!*

dare

ded Noun: battery-operated toy that is off.

dillo Noun: french fry.*

dirt Noun: shirt.

dis Noun: *I want whatever you're holding, eating, drinking, or watching.* (See MIIINE)

ded

doe

doe Noun: *toe.*

dog Noun: 1. *canine* 2. *A few years from now I will want one of these.* (See WOOF)

dough Also pronounced **dou, dour.** Noun: *door.* Verb: 1. *I want to go out* 2. *close the door* 3. *please leave and close the door from the other side.*

---

*Editor's note: Nobody knows why, but it is.

dowwn Also pronounced **da-own**. Noun or verb:
1. *put me down* 2. *I don't want to be held by this relative anymore* 3. *I'm tired of sitting in the high*

chair 4. *I want to go downstairs and play where the fragile objects are located* 5. *it's time to do something else* 6. *I am taking a step down* 7. *up.*

duk Noun: *truck.*

dukky

dukky Also pronounced **quak, ack**. Noun: *duck.*

dum Noun: your *thumb.* (Note: the word "my thumb" is indicated simply by a vigorous sucking sound.)

durtee

durtee Adjective: 1. *sticky, sloppy, and ucky* 2. *old.*
Verb: *get this out of my sight.* (See AWL-DUN, MSSSS)

dwie Verb: *time to stop with the wipes and do the
tissue thing on my bottom.*

êddy Adjective: 1. *tiny* 2. *small.* Verb: *please sing
"The Itsy-Bitsy Spider."*

e-e Noun: *dinner.* Verb: 1. *let's have dinner* 2. *I'm
starving!*

eeee Noun: 1. *Eeyore* (from *Winnie-the-Pooh*)
2. *ear.*

eeieeió

eeieeiô Noun: 1. *the way any unfamiliar song ends*
2. *a Cheerio that's fallen to the floor.*

eek Noun: 1. *mouse* 2. *what a mouse says* 3. *what a bunny says.* Adverb: *where's the cat?*

ewewyware Also pronounced
eywywre. Verb: *read Goodnight
Moon to me* (**everywhere** is the
last word in the book).

eyss Verb: *I want ice cream.*

eza Noun: *zebra.*

fshshsh Also pronounced **wissh**. Noun: *fish.*

g'en Verb: 1. *play the "Sesame Street" theme song again* 2. *down the slide once more.* (See MAWR)

goga Noun: *dog.*

grrrrr Noun: 1. *tiger* 2. *lion.*

goga

gummy guppy

gummy Also pronounced **nanni, mi-ma**. Noun: *grandma*.

guppy Also pronounced **pa-pa**. Noun: *grandpa*.

ha-choo Noun: *sound an adult makes while sneezing*. Verb: *please sneeze because it's funny (play the sneezing game)*.

hallo Also pronounced **hawo**. Verb: 1. *I want to play with the telephone* 2. *make the telephone talk*. Noun: *telephone*.

haö Noun: *hairbrush.* Verb: 1. *brush my hair* 2. *let me brush your hair.*

heeeee Also pronounced **hee-hee.** Noun: 1. *this is fun to drop* 2. *this toy is fun to stomp on.*

heidi Verb: *play hide-and-seek with me.* Adjective: *I am invisible.*

hmmmm Adjective: *I'm tired.*

holdgew Verb: See CAEOO.

honk Verb: 1. *let me squeeze your nose* 2. *please squeeze my nose.*

ide Verb: *I want to go outside.*

iide Also pronounced **died**. Noun: *park slide.* Verb: *help me up and down the park slide.*

ik Verb: 1. *(after a light to moderate fall outdoors) get this dirt (gravel, etc.) off my hands* 2. *get this food off my hands.* Adjective: *I don't like this food— see, here it comes back out of my mouth.* Noun: *mouse.*

in Also pronounced **în, 'n**. Verb: 1. *in, as in I want to go inside* 2. *I want you to go in the crib with me, now that I'm here* 3. *attach (as in attach these links)* 4. *(rarely) I want to go in my crib.*

inni Noun: *Annie. Most common reference to Raggedy Ann doll.*

Intide

intide Adverb: *where I want to be when I'm owtide.*

joos Noun: 1. *a juice cup* 2. *any liquid in a juice cup, including milk and water* 3. *soup.*

kaka

kaka Also pronounced **kæke, cakcak.** Noun:
1. *cracker* 2. *that which I intend to eat off the floor*
3. *cookie* 4. *sour-cream-and-onion potato chip.*

o

kake

kake Noun: 1. *cake* 2. *small cake crumbs that have
fallen to the floor.*

Ka-keek Noun: *"Star Trek."*

kakool Also pronounced **gababee**. Noun: *thing.*

kash Noun: *giraffe.*

kitty Also pronounced **kit**. Noun: *any large or small cat*. Also, verb: *come over here, you furry thing, I want to pull your tail.*

kksh Noun: 1. *two cars coming together* 2. *a glass breaking (accompanied by a laugh)* 3. *two stuffed animals boxing.*

knees Noun: *sneeze.*

kook Noun: *coat.* Verb: *take coat off.*

ksss Verb: 1. *one stuffed animal is kissing another* 2. *you kiss my*

Knees

stuffed animal 3. *I will kiss my stuffed animal*
4. (rarely) *you kiss me.*

kuk Noun: 1. *Cookie Monster* (from "Sesame Street") 2. *cookie.*

kwake Also pronounced **quik, gape**. Noun: *grape.*

lied Verb: *I want to go down the slide with your help.*

loud Noun: *noise.* (See NOYSE)

mæt Also pronounced **mit, meeet**. Noun: 1. *hot dog*
2. *sausage* 3. *hamburger* 4. (seldom) *Cheerios.*

maggie Noun: 1. *magazine* 2. *newspaper*
3. *catalog.* (See BUK)

ma-ma Also pronounced **mmma** Noun: 1. *the female parent* 2. *any female, including grandmothers, much to their pleasure.*

mam-mi Also pronounced **mom-mee, mi-ma**. Noun: *the female parent only.*

mana Also pronounced **mena, menema, na.** Noun: *banana.*

marki

marki Also pronounced **mahki.** Noun: (singular) *toe,* (plural) *toes,* as in *this little piggie went to market.*

mawr Also pronounced **morr, mo.** Verb: 1. *I insist you continue giving me food* 2. *continue dancing with me* 3. *continue reading to me* 4. *continue doing whatever you are doing so I don't have to go to sleep.*

me No meaning, but rhymes with a lot of words.

meow Also pronounced **kitty**. Noun: *cat*.

miiine

miiine Pronoun: 1. *that* 2. *this* 3. *everything* 4. *all objects in the house* 5. *mommy.* Verb: 1. *I want your toy* 2. *don't touch—this belongs to me* 3. *do what I say; I'm in charge.*

miki Noun: *music.* Verb: *play that song (my favorite song) again—for the twelfth time in a row.*

mi-mi,mi-mi,mi-mi Noun: *Mary had a little lamb.*

minima Also pronounced **amna**. Noun: *animal.*

mmmmmm Adverb: yes (as in *Do you want your blankie . . . milk . . . favorite stuffed animal?*). Never a response to *Are you tired?*

moo Noun: *cow.*

36

mssss

mssss Also pronounced **meschss**. Noun: *leftover food that's stuck to my hands.* Verb: 1. *see the results of my drawing (or applying food) on my arms and hands* 2. *wipe my face and hands clean right away.*

muk Also pronounced **mmm, mik, muko, mookie.** Verb: *most common meaning, I want milk.* May also mean *I want milk instantly* or *I will scream and throw my head against the floor.* Adjective: 1. *I am* thirsty 2. I don't want to eat what you are serving 3. my teeth hurt and I need something to suck on. Noun: *nipple* (See BAL)

naaaay Also pronounced **ná**. Noun: 1. *horse* 2. *naked* 3. *I want to play horsey on your back.*

na-oo Also pronounced **na-ooaa**. Verb: *stop tickling.*

nap Verb: 1. *zip my coat* 2. *button my jacket (or clothes).*

n a p

nayle Noun: 1. *nail* 2. *scissors.*

Neekok® Noun: *Kleenex.*

neekoo Noun: 1. *necklace* 2. *pull toy.*

nie-nie Noun: *another baby, person, or picture of somebody in bed.* Verb: (rarely) *I want to go to my crib.*

nite-nite Noun: *other children and animals pictured in books in a prone position.* Verb: *I am incredibly sleepy and am willing to put my head down.*

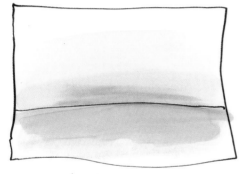

niwrrrrrrr

niwrrrrrrr Noun: 1. *sound an airplane makes*
2. *sound a stuffed animal imitating an airplane makes.*

41

nó (Said by toddlers between sixteen and twenty-four months.) Adverb: 1. *no* 2. *no* 3. *no* 4. *the only answer to a parent's question.*

noah Also pronounced **'no**. Noun: *snow*. Adjective: *white*. Verb: *I want to go sledding.* (Warning, do not confuse this word with **nó**.)

nooodowl Also pronounced **noo, noose**. Noun: 1. *spaghetti* 2. *other pasta.*

nooooo (Said by twelve- to sixteen-month-olds.) Verb: 1. *if you try, you'll be sorry* 2. *I'm not in the mood.*

nos Noun: *nose.*

eyesy

← nos

← mouth

← piggis

does →

no-way Adverb: 1. *emphatically no* 2. *urgently no* 3. *absolutely no* 4. *I am not going into the doctor's office.*

noyse Noun: *loud noise.* (See LOUD)

ö Adjective: urgent. Adverb: very.

ôn Verb: 1. *turn this battery-operated toy on* 2. *animate this toy, even though it doesn't have batteries.*

ooeeoeios Also pronounced **chê**. Noun: 1. (most common meaning) *Cheerios* Also, 2. *Oreos.*

oop Also pronounced **ooooop**.

43

Verb: 1. *used to describe a toy that is moving away such as a bath toy floating in the wrong direction or a balloon that's defying gravity* 2. *I am dropping this on the floor* 3. *look, my spoon (or your vase) dropped on the floor.*

ooshh Also pronounced **ohe**. Noun: (singular) *shoe*, (plural) *shoes.*

op Verb: *open.* (See OWUT)

ot Adjective: 1. *hot* 2. *I anticipate this to be hot* 3. *I don't want to eat that because it is too hot—just believe me* 4. *the texture of this food is all wrong.* Verb: *blow hard.*

ouf Verb: *get this peanut butter off my hands.*

ow Also pronounced **oww, awool, who-who**. Noun: *owl.* (Never means *ouch.*)

owtide Adverb: *where I want to be when I'm intide.* (See INTIDE)

owut When pronounced as **out-out-out,** very close in meaning to **waaah.** Verb: meanings include: 1. *I want to take a walk outside* 2. *I want to take a stroll outside* 3. *I want to get in the car* 4. *I want out of the high chair* 5. *let me out of here* 6. *down.*

pa Noun: *panda.*

peep-peep Noun: 1. *sound a chick makes* 2. *I hear you peeing* 3. *my diaper is wet.*

pegga Noun: *penguin.*

pigapigapa Also pronounced **piyapigapig, pee**. Noun: *pig.* (See WEE-WEE-WEE)

piggi Also pronounced **pigjie**. Noun: *toe.* (See MArKI)

pit Verb: 1. *fix my pants, they're too long and I'm tripping over them* 2. *fix my pants, they're too short and they feel funny.*

pita Noun: 1. *pizza* 2. (seldom) *Cheerios.*

pooka Verb: *I want to play peekaboo.*

'poon Noun: 1. *stick for drumming* 2. *catapult.*

P o o p

poop Also pronounced **kaka**. Noun or verb: most common meaning, *I pooped.* May also mean 1. *I will poop* 2. *there's a big poop in my diaper that has overflowed into my pants—or onto your pants* 3. *WARNING: remove me from the tub now.*

pretsi Noun: *pretzel.*

quear Also pronounced **quare**. Noun: 1. *any object that fits successfully into a shape sorter* 2. *the shape-sorter container.*

quirl Also pronounced **kurl**. Noun: 1. *squirrel* 2. *cat.*

rabbi Noun: 1. *bunny rabbit* 2. *any white, stuffed animal.* (See BUDDY)

reeda Verb: *read to me.* (See BUK)

sss Also pronounced **sss,sss, s . . . s . . . s, cee**. Noun: most common meaning, *ceiling.* Also means *ceiling fan.*

'tab Verb: *to eat or attempt to eat with a fork (as in "stab").*

ta-tu Responsive verb: *response to "Say thank you."* No actual meaning.

táweet Verb: *make the "Sesame Street" theme song play again.*

tee Noun: 1. *Tigger* (from *Winnie-the-Pooh*) 2. (also pronounced **grrrrrr**) *generic tiger* 3. *television*.

teeeeeeet Also pronounced **teeeeeeeeeeeet**. Adjective: *my teeth hurt*. (See WAAAH)

teet Also pronounced **teet, tees**. Verb: most common meaning, *brush my teeth*. May also mean *look at those teeth*.

te-ta Also pronounced **te-taak**. Noun: 1. *clock* 2. *watch*.

té-ta Verb: 1. *I want to seesaw* 2. *do not stop the seesaw*. Noun: (rarely) *seesaw*.

tik Noun: *bread stick*.

tobby Also pronounced **tubby**. Noun: *place where ducky lives*.

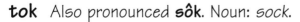

tok Also pronounced **sôk**. Noun: *sock*.

49

t-t Verb: *turn on the television.* Noun: *computer monitor.*

'tuk Adjective: *1. I'm stuck 2. my toy is stuck 3. I can't get my (article of clothing) off 4. the car seat is uncomfortable.* Verb: *let the rabbit, cat, dog, etc., out of its cage.*

uckaboo Noun: *elephant.*

uf Verb: *take this article of clothing off.*

uk Noun: *food that I don't like the taste of.*

not uk

uk

ukkle Noun: *uncle.*

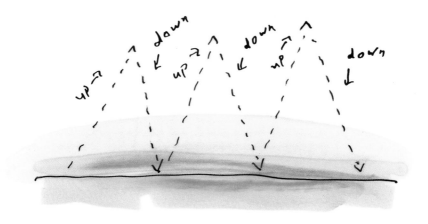

up Also pronounced **uppp, hup**. Verb: means *pick me up*. May also mean 1. *I want to go upstairs where the good toys are* 2. *pick me up for a second, then I'm going to want to be put down, then, probably I'll want to be picked up again—I'll let you know* 3. *I'm tired of walking* 4. *get me out of here!* 5. *hold me* 6. *I am taking a step up* 7. *carry my blanket on your shoulder* 8. *put me down* 9. *down.*

uuh- uuh

uuh-uuh Also pronounced **eeh-eeh, uuh**. Verb: *bring me that thing from over there.*

uuh-uuh Also pronounced **eeh-eeh, uuh**. Noun: *no, the other thing.*

waaah Also pronounced **aaaaaaaaaah**. Adjective: meanings include 1. *I hurt* 2. *I used to hurt* 3. *I want you to give me what I want* 4. *I want to continue what I was doing* 5. *I don't know what I want* 6. *I'm cranky* 7. (rarely) *out.*

wabèÿkåta Verb: *I wonder . . .* Noun.

wak Verb: 1. *I want to go walking, so don't take the stroller, but after a block or two I will want to be carried* 2. *I'm tired of being cooped up inside and want to go out* 3. *I'm tired of being cooped up inside, but don't want to go out.* (Never: *I want to walk indoors.*)

wa-wa Also pronounced **wa**. Noun: *water (as a statement of fact)*. Adjective: 1. *I'm thirsty* 2. *I want to swim.*

way Verb: *go away.*

weeeeee Verb: *pick me up and whirl me around.*

wee-wee-wee Also pronounced **wee-hom**. Noun: *sound a pig makes (from this little piggie went wee-wee-wee all the way home).*

whet Noun: 1. *water* 2. *milk or juice that has been spilled on a shirt* 3. *rain* 4. *melting snow* 5. *swimming pool* 6. *diaper wipe.*

whipe Noun: 1. *diaper wipe* 2. *Kleenex.* Verb: 1. *please change my diaper* 2. *my bear made a poo-poo and I need to clean him* 3. *I want to pretend to clean the table.*

whut Adjective: *I'm wet.* Verb: *come splash in the puddle with me.* Noun: 1. *umbrella* 2. *diaper wipes* 3. *rain.*

wing Verb: 1. *I want to get in the swing* 2. *I want to stay in the swing forever.*

woof Also pronounced **uarf**. Noun: *dog*. (See DOG)

woof-woof Also pronounced **uarf-uarf, oof-oof**. Noun: *sound a dog makes.*

woosh Noun: 1. *slide* 2. *swing.*

woo-woo Noun: *fire engine.*

wug Noun: *the center of target in the Cheerio-tossing game.*

wush Noun: 1. *bath time.*

PART 2

An English-Baby
Dictionary

Your baby doesn't understand you? You say, "Come over
here Rachel," and Rachel keeps on a heading toward the
Doberman that's running loose down the street?

It's useful to point out that what's a complete
sentence to an adult translates into a single word in
Baby-English: infants understand our sentences as a
single thought, which is, after all, what we were taught
sentences are. What takes ordinary English a sentence or
more to say can be distilled to a few sounds in baby-talk.

Parents, obviously, have a lot to do with the words their
children learn and understand. Sometimes these

unplanned vocabulary lessons can have unpredictable—and funny—consequences. For about six months, every time my wife and I attached the tray to Karen's high chair, we remarked, "Tray [*très*] means 'very' in French." Not that we were trying to teach her a foreign language (it's hard enough to teach that the vase is not a toy), but this just became oft-repeated household humor. Periodially, we'd ask Karen, "Tray means 'very' in . . . ?" and she would respond, "French!" Amazed the grandparents, at least. Well, one day we put Karen in her chair and she started asking for the *french*. For about five minutes we had no idea what she wanted—the *bench? the wrench?*—until we finally figured it out. Well, for Karen *french* now means "tray."

But it's not entirely your baby's fault that he or she doesn't understand you. After all, the two of you speak a different language. Part 2 of *Baby-English* lets you appreciate the difference between what you say and what your baby understands.

WARNING

It is highly recommended that you do not use any of the following words in the presence of an eight- to twenty-four-month-old without carefully evaluating the ramifications.

cookie
milk
out
outside
peekaboo
stroller

absolutely not Verb: try again.

aunt Noun: 1. *wet, slobbering kiss* 2. *thick, humid hug.*

baby food Noun: 1. *too sour* 2. *too sweet* 3. *too bland* 4. *too ucky.*

baby-sitter Noun: 1. *someone who has kidnapped or taken away Mommy and Daddy forever* 2. *wonderful older baby who lets me stay up as long as I want.*

bath Noun: *splash time.*

be careful Verb: *frighten Mommy and Daddy.*

bed Noun: *place where there are all sorts of fun, unusual objects, including Mommy and Daddy.*

beddy-bye Noun: See SLEEPY TIME.

be nice to the baby Verb: *that baby is going to hit or push me.*

bib Adjective: *uncomfortable*. Noun: 1. *something too sour is coming* 2. *time to play 'poon* (See Baby-English section). Verb: *to strangle*.

book Noun: *a tear-out-card toy*.

boom-boom Noun: *sound another baby makes when it falls*. (See BOOM-BOOM in Baby-English section)

bracelet Noun: *teething ring.*

breakfast Noun: 1. *"Sesame Street" time*
2. *trapped-in-high-chair time.*

bye-bye Verb: *flap hands.*

can you show Grandma how you . . . Verb: *keep absolutely silent and still.*

car Noun: 1. *big out* 2. *ride-on toy* 3. *toy car* 4. *a mystery trip.*

car seat Adjective: *trapped.*

cards (*deck of cards*) Noun: *tossing toys.*

clown Noun: *scary monster.*

coffee Noun: *brown water.*

computer Noun: 1. *great toy with great colors and great cartoons that Daddy and Mommy control* 2. *great toy with great colors and great cartoons that I play with when Mommy and Daddy aren't around.*

cookie Noun: *the good stuff in the box.*

cracker Noun: *potato chip.*

crayon Verb: *let's change the color of the wall.*

crib Noun: *place where there is no Mommy and Daddy.*

daddy Noun: *the other parent, whom you rarely see around the changing table, has been summoned to change your diaper. This may not happen again for a while.*

daddy's here Noun: *1. playtime 2. time to watch TV 3. (seldom) time to play the upside-down game.*

desk Noun: *climbing structure.*

diaper Noun: 1. *a paper toy* 2. *pants I can practice taking off by myself.*

diaper table Noun: *torture rack.*

doctor Noun: *pain.*

d-o-c-t-o-r Noun: *?-?-?-?-?-?*

does it hurt? Verb: cry louder.

does. it - hurt?

don't. eat- that- off -
the- floor

don't eat that off the floor Adjective: what fine weather we're having.

71

don't play with your food Verb: *invent a new game to play with the food.*

don't push Verb: *push.*

don't put that in your mouth Adjective: *yummy.*

don't splash Verb: *splash.*

do you want to go for a drive? Noun: *place where I will take my entire nap for the day.*

do you want to use the potty? Also pronounced **potty time.** Verb: *time to poop on the floor.*

eat Verb: *1. throw 2. spit out after chewing 3. fling.*

eyeglasses Noun: *a permanently available toy, within easy reach.*

flower Noun: *vegetable.*

fly Verb: *niwrrrrrrrr.*

food Noun: *Silly Putty.*

fork Noun: *spoon.*

garbage Noun: *toy.*

fly

give Daddy (or Mommy) a kiss Verb: *say "no."*
(See PLEASE)

a kiss

give that to Mommy Verb: *put it in mouth.*

Grandma's Noun: *new toy.*

hair wash Verb: *fun time in the bath ends.*

hat Noun: *thing up there—what is it?—get it off.*

hello Verb: *do anything you want.*

hold my hand Verb: *run.*

hot Verb: *I can look at the food, but can't eat it.*

I'll be right back Adverb: *you're going away for-ever . . .*

it's cold outside Adjective: *hot.* (See SNOWSUIT)

later Adjective: *never.* (See NOT NOW)

laundry basket Noun: *amusement-park ride.*

let me put your shoes on—let's go! Verb: *time to play run-and-chase-around-the-house.*

let me tie your shoes Verb: *kick.*

let me wipe your face Verb: *swivel head from side to side.*

let's get you dressed (See WHAT DO YOU WANT TO WEAR TODAY)

little boy Noun: *what people keep calling me even though I'm not.* (See LITTLE GIRL)

little girl Noun: *a baby who is in some way different from a boy, but I don't know how.*

living room Noun: *1. playroom 2. learn-to-walk place.*

look Verb: *look this way while I take away whatever's in your hands.*

look out! Verb: *something interesting is about to happen.*

77

loud Verb: *cover your ears.*

meet your new baby brother Noun: *the end of the universe, as I know it.*

M-i-c, k-e-y Verb: *yell "Mouse!"*

Mickey Mouse Noun: *bear with a black hat.*

milk Noun: *1. breakfast 2. lunch 3. dinner 4. in-between snack 5. three A.M. snack.* Verb: *(occasionally) a way to test that gravity still works.*

mittens Noun: *handcuffs.*

Mommy Noun: *the other tall person who does my diaper.*

mystery novel Verb: *tear-out-the-back-page toy.*

necklace Noun: *marble set.* (See NEEKOO in Baby-English section)

newspaper Noun: 1. *what Mommy and Daddy do when they won't play with me* 2. *rip-up toy.*

niwrrrrrrrr

niwrrrrrrrr Noun: 1. *a spoonful of food circling overhead* 2. *sound a parent makes trying to manipulate a stuffed animal and make it appear to fly so as to mollify a screaming baby.* (See DIAPER TABLE)

no also pronounced **NO.** Noun: 1. *lamp* 2. *vase* 3. *door hinge.*

not now Adverb: *never.* (See LATER)

now Verb: *stop.*

out Noun: 1. *the place where the dogs and cats roam* 2. *the place where squirrels are* 3. *the place where other babies live.*

outside (See OUT)

oven Noun: *secret place.*

peek a boo Verb: *watch Mommy and Daddy slap themselves in the face.*

play group Noun: *time to push and be pushed.*

please Verb: *say no.*

please eat Verb: *clamp mouth shut and sway head from side to side.*

Pooh Noun: 1. *star of Winnie-the-Pooh* 2. *the stuffed animal that's not in the room with me.*

radio Noun: 1. *loud machine* 2. *place where Raffi (or Wee Sing) lives.*

refrigerator Noun: *place where the milk hides.*

remote control Also pronounced **klicker**. Noun:
1. *teether* 2. *thing that makes the tee-tee make
pictures* 3. *thing that when I hold and press it makes
Mommy and Daddy scream and wiggle.*

restaurant Verb: *can't watch TV while eating.*

ring-around-the-rosy Verb: *for the next thirty
minutes, run around in circles holding hands.*

rock Noun: *hard, sucking candy.*

rug Noun: *target for oeeios and other food.*

shower head Noun: *rainmaker.*

siren Verb: *hold hands over ears.*

sky Verb: *look up.*

sleepy time Noun: *extra playtime.*

snowsuit Adjective: *hot.*

socks Noun: *chance of being tickled.*

spoon Noun: *catapult.*

stab Noun: *fork, as in Do you want to use a fork to stab your food?*

stop Verb: *no known meaning.*

stop kicking (said to a baby on the changing table) Noun: *chance for one last solid kick in the midsection.*

stroller Noun: *scenery-viewing machine.* Adverb: *they're not going to let me walk.*

taxes Verb: *watch Daddy kick the wall and pound the table.*

telephone Noun: 1. *toy with all the buttons to push* 2. *toy that makes Mommy and Daddy act funny when I push the buttons* 3. *hammer.*

television Noun: 1. *cartoons* 2. *flat people.*

that's Daddy's . . . Verb: *time to play hide-and-seek.*

that's the cat's food Verb: *cat likes to eat this + I like the cat = I can eat this, too.*

the scale Noun: *the cold, scary torture-thing.*

this is not a toy Verb: *they're taking away my toy.*

time to come out of the tub Adjective: *unpleasant.*

time to go Verb: *must stop playing and will never be allowed to play games again.*

tree Noun: *place where the quirls are.* (See QUIRL in Baby-English section)

vase Noun: *do-it-yourself jigsaw puzzle.*

VCR Noun: 1. *storage compartment for toys* 2. *food-storage container.*

wading pool Noun: 1. *yes place!* 2. *potty.*

wastebasket Noun: *toy box.*

watch out for the puddle Verb: *go splash.*

we're home Verb: *Mommy and Daddy have rematerialized.*

what do you want to wear today? Verb: *time to throw the clothes around.*

what's the matter? Verb: *don't stop crying no matter what.*

yaaaaaaaaah Verb: *look at all that brown stuff floating in the bath.*

yuk Noun: *an object from the sidewalk.*